KU-555-774

WITHDRAWN
FROM STOCK

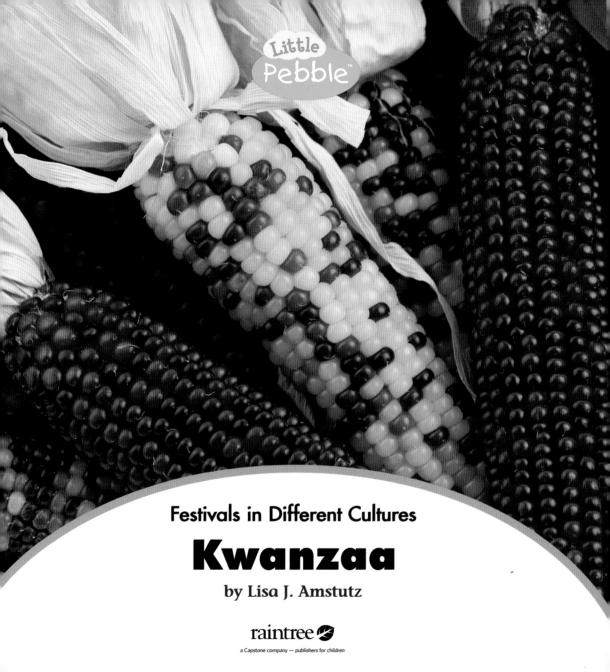

Little Pebble™

Festivals in Different Cultures

Kwanzaa

by Lisa J. Amstutz

raintree

a Capstone company — publishers for children

Raintree is an imprint of Capstone Global Library Limited, a company incorporated in England and Wales having its registered office at 264 Banbury Road, Oxford, OX2 7DY – Registered company number: 6695582

www.raintree.co.uk
myorders@raintree.co.uk

Text © Capstone Global Library Limited 2017
The moral rights of the proprietor have been asserted.

All rights reserved. No part of this publication may be reproduced in any form or by any means (including photocopying or storing it in any medium by electronic means and whether or not transiently or incidentally to some other use of this publication) without the written permission of the copyright owner, except in accordance with the provisions of the Copyright, Designs and Patents Act 1988 or under the terms of a licence issued by the Copyright Licensing Agency, Saffron House, 6–10 Kirby Street, London EC1N 8TS (www.cla.co.uk). Applications for the copyright owner's written permission should be addressed to the publisher.

Edited by Jill Kalz
Designed by Julie Peters
Picture research by Pam Mitsakos
Production by Steve Walker

Printed and bound in China

ISBN 978 1 4747 3795 1
20 19 18 17 16
10 9 8 7 6 5 4 3 2 1

British Library Cataloguing in Publication Data
A full catalogue record for this book is available from the British Library.

Acknowledgements
We would like to thank the following for permission to reproduce photographs:
Capstone Press: Capstone Studio/Karon Dubke, cover; Dreamstime: Scott Griessel, 9; Getty Images: Hill Street Studios, 5; Newscom: Hill Street Studios Blend Images, 15, John VanBeekum/MCT, 7; Shutterstock: Candus Camera, 1, 22, 24, back cover, Enraged, 10, Pichugin Dmitry, 13, Svetlana Foote, 14, Timothy R. Nichols, 17, Uber Images, 11, xtock, 8 inset; The Image Works: E.A. Kennedy, 21, Thinkstock: Jupiterimages, 3, Purestock, 19
Every effort has been made to contact copyright holders of material reproduced in this book. Any omissions will be rectified in subsequent printings if notice is given to the publisher.

All the Internet addresses (URLs) given in this book were valid at the time of going to press. However, due to the dynamic nature of the Internet, some addresses may have changed, or sites may have changed or ceased to exist since publication. While the author and publisher regret any inconvenience this may cause readers, no responsibility for any such changes can be accepted by either the author or the publisher.

CORK CITY LIBRARY
9352914

Contents

What is Kwanzaa?

Come together.

Light the candles.

Share stories.

Kwanzaa is here!

Kwanzaa is an
African-American
holiday. It is a time
to give thanks.

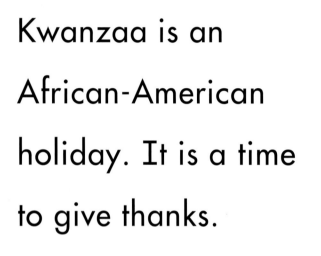

Kwanzaa starts 26th December.

It lasts seven days.

Let's get ready

People make gifts.

They set out seven symbols.

Each symbol has a story.

The stories come from Africa.

A mat holds fruit and nuts.

Each child gets an ear of corn.

Everyone shares the unity cup.

The kinara holds seven candles.

One is black. Three are red.

Three are green.

Kwanzaa begins

Families light one candle each night. They talk. They share ways to help one another.

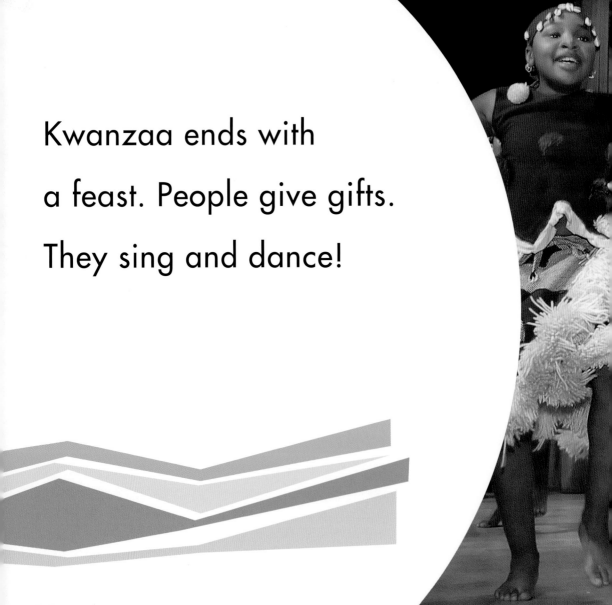

Kwanzaa ends with
a feast. People give gifts.
They sing and dance!

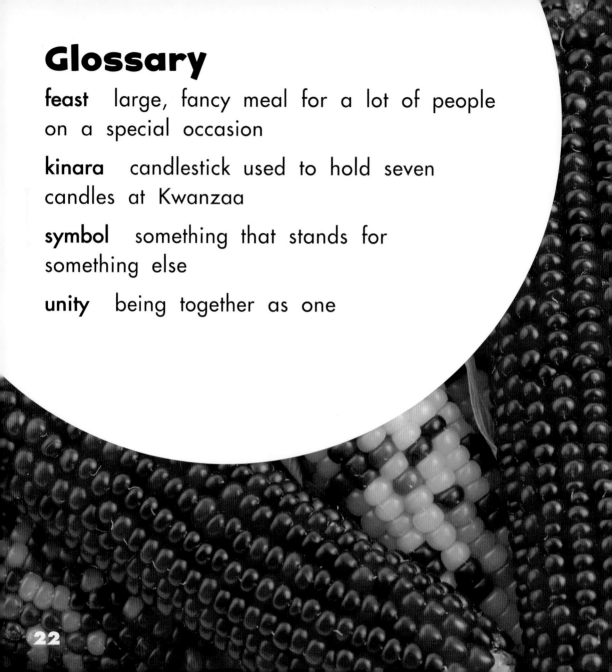

Glossary

feast   large, fancy meal for a lot of people on a special occasion

kinara   candlestick used to hold seven candles at Kwanzaa

symbol   something that stands for something else

unity   being together as one

Read more

Kwanzaa (Holidays and Festivals), Rebecca Rissman (Heinemann Library, 2011)

Kwanzaa (Story of Our Holidays), Joanna Ponto (Enslow Publishing, 2016)

My First Kwanzaa (My First Holiday), Karen Katz (Square Fish, 2014)

Websites

www.activityvillage.co.uk/kwanzaa
Learn about Kwanzaa and how it's celebrated. Play games, enjoy crafts and read stories all about Kwanzaa!

www.fun-facts.org.uk/holidays/kwanzaa.htm
Discover fun facts about Kwanzaa!

CORK CITY LIBRARY

Comprehension questions

1. Where do the Kwanzaa stories come from?

2. Name the three colors of the kinara candles.

Index

24